QUESTIONS AND ANSWERS ABOUT SHARKS

by **ANN McGOVERN** ■ illustrated by **PAM JOHNSON**

SCHOLASTIC INC.

New York   Toronto   London   Auckland   Sydney

CONTENTS

How long have sharks been around? 4

Do all sharks look alike? 6

When do sharks attack people? 8

Are all sharks dangerous? 10

What sharks are most dangerous? 12

What sharks are harmless? 13

What is the biggest shark and what is the smallest shark? 14

Where do sharks live? 16

What are some of the deepwater sharks? 17

What do baby sharks look like? 20

How does the mother shark care for her pups? 21

Do sharks eat other sharks? 22

What else do sharks eat? 22

How often do sharks have to eat? 24

How do sharks find their food? 25

Is there anything that keeps sharks away? 28

How do sharks use their teeth? 30

What do sharks' teeth look like? 32

Do sharks have enemies? 33

Do sharks have friends? 34

Do big sharks ever stop swimming? 36

Do sharks really sleep? 39

How fast do sharks swim? 39

Are sharks in danger of disappearing? 40

What good are sharks? 42

What do scientists want to find out about sharks? 44

How long have sharks been around?

There were sharks about 400 million years ago. Before there were dinosaurs, there were sharks.

Dinosaurs died out about 70 million years ago. But the sharks lived on.

Sharks of long, long ago looked much like most sharks of today.

Here is a picture of a shark.

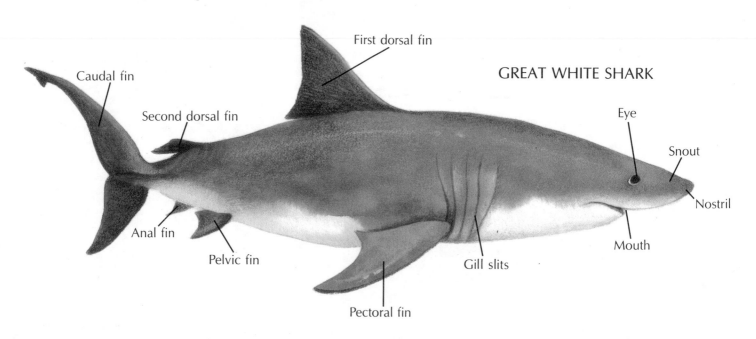

First dorsal fin

GREAT WHITE SHARK

Caudal fin

Second dorsal fin

Eye

Snout

Nostril

Anal fin

Mouth

Pelvic fin

Gill slits

Pectoral fin

A shark is a fish. It lives in water and breathes through gills like all fish.

Most fish have skeletons made of true bones. But sharks are not bony fish. Their skeletons are made of something softer called *cartilage*. (The "bones" in the end of your nose are made of cartilage.)

Most sharks give birth to live baby sharks instead of laying eggs.

A shark's skin looks smooth and slippery. If you stroke a shark one way, it will feel smooth. But if you stroke it the other way, ouch! Your hand may be cut and bleeding.

A shark's body is covered with a hard material that looks — and feels — like bits of sharp teeth.

Do all sharks look alike?

No. There are at least 370 different kinds of sharks.
Here is what some of them look like.

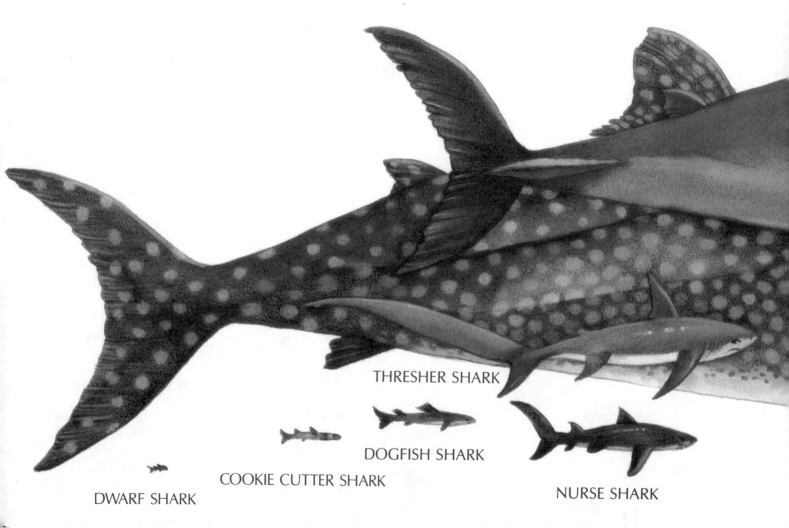

THRESHER SHARK

DOGFISH SHARK

COOKIE CUTTER SHARK

DWARF SHARK

NURSE SHARK

SIXGILL

MEGAMOUTH

BASKING SHARK

WHALE SHARK

When do sharks attack people?

People are not normally part of a shark's menu. There are far fewer shark attacks on people than you might think. Throughout the world, about one hundred people are attacked each year. But only twenty-five die, mostly from loss of blood — not from being eaten. Of course, that's twenty-five deaths too many.

Most shark attacks on humans are of the bite-and-spit-out type. It may be that the shark is frightened and takes a bite as a warning to the stranger to get out of his way. Perhaps one bite convinces the shark that a human is not good to eat.

Some scientists say that most attacks are cases of mistaken identity. Humans are about the same size as seals, a favorite food of the great white shark.

A fish struggling on a fisherman's line sets the water in motion. The water vibrates. These vibrations bring sharks swimming in from far away. The smell of blood in the water attracts sharks, too. So it's not wise to hold a bleeding, struggling fish in the water. The shark might aim for the fish but bite the person by mistake.

Even harmless sharks will sometimes attack if they are annoyed. Once a diver was showing off to his friends. He caught a nurse shark and held it by the tail. Suddenly the nurse shark turned and bit him on the leg.

Scientists say the chance of being killed by a shark

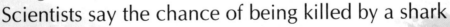
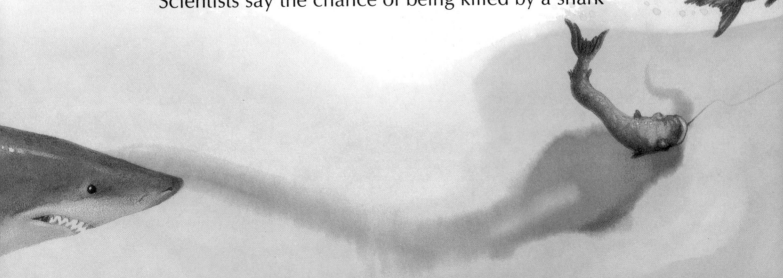

is far less than that of dying from a bee sting, a snake bite, lightning, or even a pig! It's true. More people in the United States are killed by pigs than by sharks.

Sharks have a lot more to fear from humans. People eat about a hundred million sharks a year. Imagine the scary movies sharks could make about us!

Are all sharks dangerous?

No.

Of the 370 different kinds of sharks in the world, fewer than 70 are dangerous; that's about twenty percent.

Most sharks seem to be afraid of people.

Many scuba divers say that the sharks they meet swim away from *them!*

HAMMERHEAD SHARKS

What sharks are most dangerous?

Some people call the *great white shark* "white death"! It is the most dangerous shark, but hardly anyone ever sees it. It does not often come into shallow waters where most people swim.

The *bull shark* does come into shallow water. It is the only shark that goes from the sea into some rivers.

Other dangerous sharks are the *mako shark,* the *blue shark,* the *tiger shark,* and the strange-looking *hammerhead shark* — although many divers have swum with these sharks and the sharks just kept swimming by.

The *carpet shark* (sometimes called *wobbegong shark*) is found in Australia. It rests on the bottom of the sea by day. Its colors look so much like part of the sea bottom that sometimes a swimmer steps right on the shark. Then the shark is likely to attack the swimmer.

What sharks are harmless?

It would take pages and pages to list all the harmless sharks in the world. There would be more than 300 different kinds in the list.

The biggest fish in the world is a *whale shark,* and it is not likely to attack anyone. Swimmers have even taken rides on the backs of whale sharks. Whale sharks feed on small fish and on *plankton* — the tiniest living things in the sea.

Another harmless giant is the *basking shark.* Its teeth are less than ½″ long, and it never bites people.

Sometimes a harmless shark turns mean.

Sometimes one kind of shark is more dangerous in one place than in another. Scientists do not always know why.

Basking sharks swim slowly through thick plankton with their mouths open. As water passes through their mouths, tiny fish and plankton get caught in the *gill rakers,* a kind of strainer.

What is the biggest shark and what is the smallest shark?

The whale shark is the biggest shark. It is also the biggest fish in the world. It grows to 50 feet long — bigger than two big station wagons. It can weigh more than 15 tons! That's how much six big cars weigh.

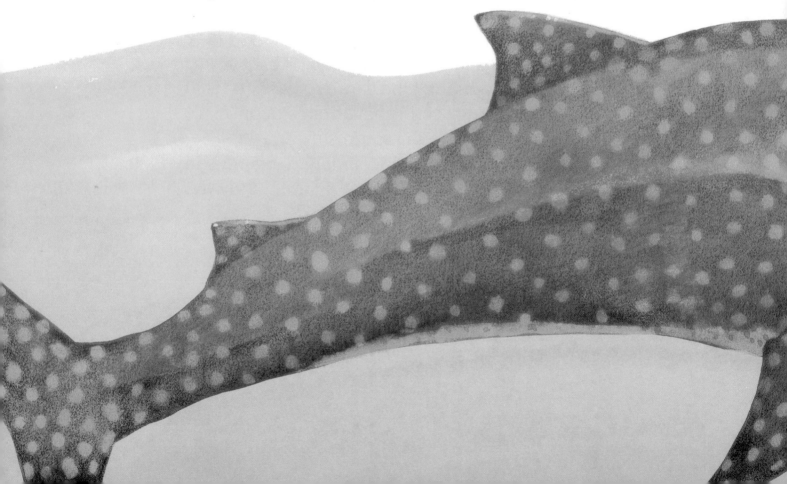

One adult shark can fit in the palm of your hand.
It is only five inches long.
The Japanese named it
t s u r a n a g a k o b i t o z a m e.
The word means "the dwarf shark with a long
face." The name on this page is as long as the shark!

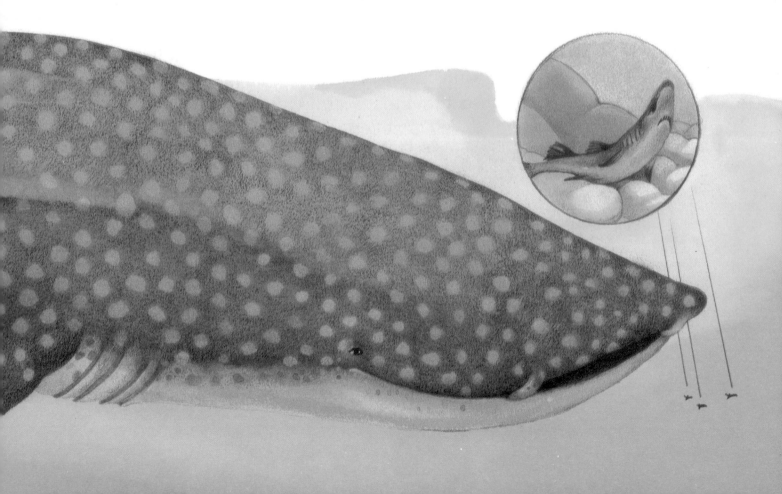

Where do sharks live?

Sharks live in waters all over the world. Almost all sharks live in oceans.

A few sharks live in warm rivers and bays. The bull shark sometimes goes back and forth from the ocean to the rivers — mostly in the warmer places of the world.

Sharks are found in warm waters and in cold waters. Many kinds even live in icy waters.

Some scientists think that warm-water sharks may move to cooler waters at certain times of the year.

And there are sharks in the deep, deep sea that no one had ever seen alive until the 1980s. In small submarines called submersibles, and with remotely operated cameras, scientists have been able to explore, study, and make videos and pictures of sharks that live as deep as 6,000 feet undersea.

Scientists agree that the deep sea is the newest frontier of discovery.

What are some of the deepwater sharks?

The *Pacific sleeper shark* may reach the size of a city bus, bigger than the great white shark.

Newly discovered tiny sharks called *deepwater dwarf dogsharks* are found mostly in the Caribbean Sea. It is believed that they hunt in packs, like the wild dogs they were named for. In this way they can attack victims as big as whales. Octopus beaks have been found in their stomachs.

A *false cat shark* was filmed for the first time in the 1980s; so were the biggest living *sixgill sharks*. Other sharks that were recently filmed are *gulper sharks*, *big fin gummy sharks*, *cigar sharks*, and the strange *megamouth*.

In 1976, the first megamouth was discovered when it accidentally swallowed a sea anchor off Hawaii. By 1994, four more megamouths had been found around the world. You can guess by this shark's name that it has a gigantic mouth! It is believed that light from its huge mouth attracts the plankton it feeds upon, just as moths are attracted to light.

Male megamouths get as big as 17 feet. The five discovered by 1994 were all males. Females may be bigger. Megamouth is one of the most mysterious sharks in the world. Scientists want to know more about it.

The *green-eyed cookie-cutter shark*, which can be small (two feet long), medium (four to five feet), or large (20 feet), is another newly discovered species. At night the cookie cutter shark swims up from the deep to the surface to feed on large fish, even dolphins, seals, and whales. It sinks its teeth tightly into its victim. Then it spins around, cutting a perfect circle. When the victim tries to get away, the cookie cutter hangs on with its fleshy lips. Its big muscular tongue pulls back, forming a vacuum, and sucks out the "cookie" — a plug of skin and flesh.

What do baby sharks look like?

Shark babies are fully formed when they are born. They look like small copies of adult sharks.

Shark babies are called *pups*.

Some sharks have only two pups at a time. Other sharks can have as many as 100.

A tiger shark has about 40 or 50 pups. Each one is about two feet long — about as long as a full-grown cat.

How does the mother shark care for her pups?

She doesn't. Shark pups are born knowing how to swim. They are born with teeth, and they can defend themselves right away!

A mother shark does not eat right after her pups are born. This is probably a good thing for the shark pups. What if she ate some of her babies?

Soon the mother shark swims away from her pups.

Some pups are born in shallow waters. When the mother shark leaves, the pups stay behind to eat and grow. When winter comes, they may travel to warmer waters. No adult shark travels with them.

Do sharks eat other sharks?

Yes. Small sharks are often part of a large shark's meal. And some large sharks, like the tiger shark, eat other large sharks.

When the water is churned up, the vibrations in the water can start a "feeding frenzy." Sharks race in from all directions.

They go wild. They have been known to rush at a ship's propeller and to chew up wooden oars of a boat.

If a shark is injured, other sharks will turn on it. They may attack it and eat it even if it is one of their own kind.

What else do sharks eat?

A shark's favorite food is freshly killed fish — or a dolphin if the shark can find a dead or a wounded one.

Healthy dolphins and many big fish are usually too fast for a shark to catch. But when these creatures are wounded or dead — or are too young to defend themselves — they may become a meal for some shark.

The great white shark can eat big creatures. One 15-foot great white shark was captured with two whole sandbar sharks inside it. Each of them was as big as a grown person.

The largest sharks — the basking shark and the whale shark — like tiny bits of food. They filter plankton out of the water. Megamouth is a filter feeder, too. The enormous mouths of these three sharks take in huge amounts of plankton.

The tiger shark will swallow almost anything that will fit into its mouth. Inside one tiger shark, fishermen found a leather wallet (without any money), a broken alarm clock, and a collection of nuts and bolts.

Hammerhead sharks will often eat stingrays. The tail of a stingray has one or two poisonous spines, but that doesn't seem to bother the hammerhead!

How often do sharks have to eat?

Most sharks can go for a long time without food — because of their liver.

A shark's liver is full of oil and fats. These oils and fats can keep a shark going for a long time — sometimes for months.

How do sharks find their food?

A shark uses all of its senses to find its food — smelling, seeing, hearing, and touching.

A shark's sense of smell is very sharp. It can follow the smell of blood across a mile of ocean and find exactly where it's coming from.

Sharks use their eyes to hunt for food, too. Some sharks can see 50 feet away in clear water. (Eight motorcycles in a row measure about 50 feet.)

Sharks see better in dim light than in bright light. Maybe that's why they hunt for food mostly at dawn and after sunset, when they can outsee most other fish.

Even more important to the shark than its eyes are the sensory pores located at the front of its head. These pores, called *ampullae of Lorenzini*, help the shark detect and home in on prey.

You can't see a shark's ears because they are inside the shark's head.

Scientists made tests to learn about the shark's sense of hearing. The scientists put a microphone into the water. They taped the sounds made by a big fish that was thrashing around.

Then they played back the tapes through underwater loudspeakers. Sharks rushed in and swam directly to where the sounds were coming from.

Every shark has a kind of combination sense of hearing and sense of feeling. This is due to its *lateral line system*, which runs along the shark's body and onto its head. The lateral line system helps the shark hear and feel vibrations made by a fish moving as far as 100 feet away.

A shark will sometimes bump into a fish before he eats it. Scientists say sharks have special cells in their skin. By bumping into a fish, a shark can "feel" if that fish would be good to eat.

The tail of a thresher shark is half as long as its body. It uses its long tail to stun small fish. Then it turns and eats the fish.

Is there anything that keeps sharks away?

Yes. It's a small flat fish called the Moses sole that lives in the Red Sea. Milky-white fluid oozes from its fins. Dr. Eugenie Clark tested the Moses sole with a shark in the lab. When she put the little fish into the shark tank, the shark opened its jaws wide to gobble it up. And its jaws stayed stuck wide open. The white fluid from the Moses sole kept the shark from closing its jaws.

Then Dr. Clark washed the skin of the Moses sole with alcohol. Again she dropped the fish into the shark tank. In no time the Moses sole was eaten by the shark. Washing the fish with alcohol took away the mucus on its skin with the poison in it. Cooking also destroys its poison.

Dr. Clark wondered how sharks in the sea would react to the Moses sole. She baited long lines with different kinds of fish, including the Moses sole. She put the lines into the sea. At night, sharks swam up from the deep. They ate up all the little fish wriggling on the lines — but they didn't eat the Moses sole!

Scientists made more experiments. They put a small shark in a tank along with the fluid from one Moses sole. In six hours, the shark was dead!

The poison from the little Moses sole is the best chemical shark repellent to be discovered so far. A thimbleful of the milky fluid could keep hungry sharks away for many hours — 18 hours in one of the tests.

But some other tests showed that two pounds of the fluid would have to be poured into the sea every hour to really protect a diver. So scientists are still looking for something cheap, effective, and safe that keeps sharks away.

How do sharks use their teeth?

Sharks use their teeth to bite and tear and crush food, but they do not use their teeth for chewing.

Most sharks have more than four rows of teeth. The teeth in the front row do all the work. New teeth move up from the row behind. The new teeth push out the teeth in the front row.

Sharks can grow a new set of teeth every two weeks! In ten years, a tiger shark may use up more than 5,000 teeth!

A great white shark may attack from below. Its powerful jaws snap shut on its prey. The shark's body shakes violently from side to side. Its sharp teeth tear off as much as 15 pounds of flesh.

What do sharks' teeth look like?

Every kind of shark has different teeth. A scientist can look at a single tooth and know what kind of shark it came from.

Some sharks have teeth that are good for cutting or grasping or crushing.

This is what the tooth of a great white shark looks like.

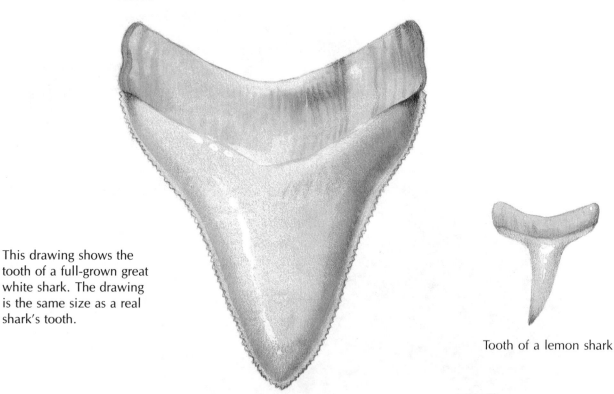

This drawing shows the tooth of a full-grown great white shark. The drawing is the same size as a real shark's tooth.

Tooth of a lemon shark

Do sharks have enemies?

Some sharks kill other sharks. But it is people who are the sharks' greatest enemies.

People use different parts of sharks for different things.

Sharkskin is stronger than cowhide. Shark skins are treated like leather and used to make shoes and belts and pocketbooks.

Shark teeth are used to make jewelry.

Shark fins are used to make soup.

Shark meat is eaten by people all over the world.

Tooth of a mako shark

Tooth of a tiger shark

Teeth of a nurse shark

Do sharks have friends?

Maybe you wouldn't call them friends, but two kinds of fish travel with sharks all the time.

The *pilot fish* travels with the shark.

When the shark eats, the pilot fish gets the scraps. And the pilot fish is protected from big fish who don't dare get too close to the shark.

What does the shark get in return? Nothing. People once thought that pilot fish led sharks to the fish they feed on. They don't. Sharks have no trouble finding their own food.

Remoras travel with sharks, too. A remora has a disc on the top of its head. It uses this disc to fasten itself to sharks.

When the shark eats, remoras swim off to pick up the food scraps. Then they come back to the shark and attach themselves to its body again. Many sharks carry two or more remoras.

The remora gets a free ride and it gets food, too. What does the shark get in return? It gets a cleaning. The remora picks off tiny parasites from the shark.

When two very different kinds of animals live together in this way, scientists call it *symbiosis* (say sim-be-*oh*-sis). Symbiosis simply means "living together."

Do big sharks ever stop swimming?

Until 1972, everyone thought big sharks had to swim all the time so that water would be flowing over their gills constantly. Water contains oxygen that all sharks need to stay alive. It was thought that if they didn't keep moving, the sharks would drown.

Then, in 1972, a Mexican photographer discovered reef sharks in an underwater cave, 67 feet below the surface, in a sleeplike state.

Dr. Eugenie Clark studied "sleeping" sharks in underwater caves in Mexico, Japan, and the Red Sea.

She and her assistants noticed that the sharks in the caves were very clean, free of the tiny parasites that grow on big fish. They saw remoras cleaning parasites off the sharks.

Dr. Clark wondered if the caves could be cleaning stations for sharks.

In the open seas, most sharks do swim without stopping. They use their tails or caudal fins for power and for sudden change of direction, too. Pectoral fins are the sharks' front fins, used for steering, turning, and braking.

Do sharks really sleep?

The more the sharks in the caves were studied, the more it was found that they didn't sleep the way humans sleep. The sharks' eyes followed the divers' every move.

How fast do sharks swim?

It's almost impossible to measure how fast a shark swims in the open seas. In captivity, sharks are known to swim up to three miles an hour. Scientists think that sharks in the oceans swim ten times faster. And they can swim even faster in short bursts of speed. A blue shark was clocked at 43 miles per hour when it was in an attack position.

Are sharks in danger of disappearing?

Sharks have been around for 400 million years, and it's likely that they will be around for millions more.

Baby sharks can take care of themselves. So a large number grow to be adult sharks.

But some people are getting worried about the great numbers of sharks that are hunted.

Who eats sharks? Larger sharks. And humans. The fins and tails of great white sharks are used to make soup in Asia. People in Hong Kong pay $50 for a bowl of shark-fin soup. So shark hunters kill the great whites for money. They cut off the fins and tails and sell them. They sell the jaws and big teeth, too. Then they dump the rest of the shark in the sea.

Shark expert Dr. Samuel Gruber says that "great whites are in trouble everywhere they go, which is almost everywhere in the world."

Other sharks living along the coasts are hunted widely, too, including the lemon shark, tiger shark, and nurse shark. In 1994, about 370,000 sharks were killed. So many shark deaths are causing a serious drop in their population.

Dr. Gruber sums it up. "There's so much that's fascinating about sharks that to have them killed off before we've explored the wonders of their biology and ecology, especially in ignorance and just to make a quick buck, is a crime."

What good are sharks?

The shark's immune system is one of the most re-markable in the animal kingdom. In their natural habitat, sharks can ward off almost any disease, in-cluding cancer. What scientists learn from sharks can be of great medical help to people. Many scientists are working with sharks, trying to find new ways to cure diseases.

Artificial skin made of shark cartilage may help people with serious burns.

In many parts of the world, people have already discovered that shark meat is good for you and good to eat. Besides, it has no bones to watch out for.

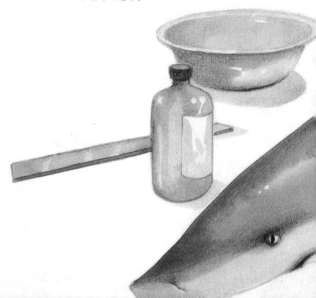

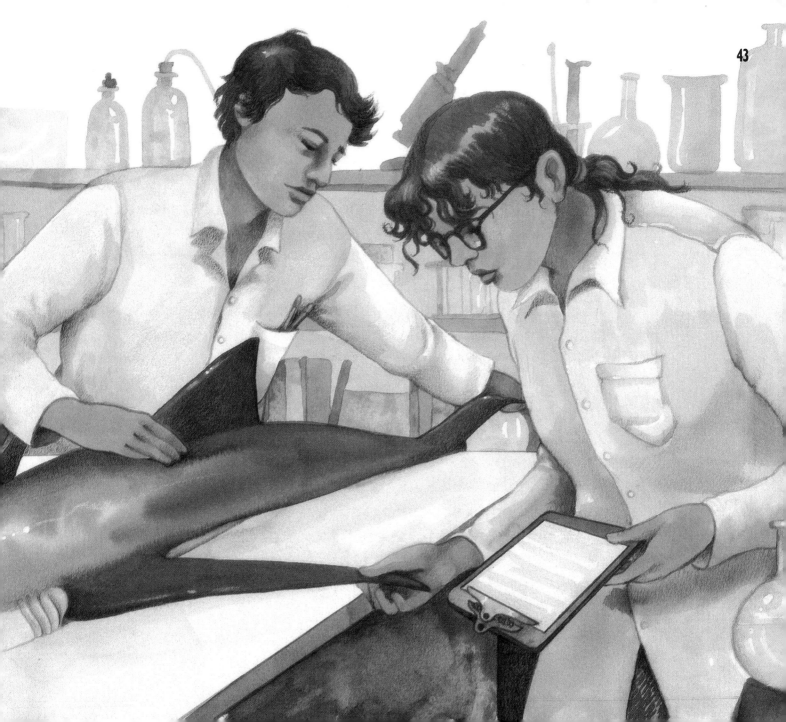

What do scientists want to find out about sharks?

There is still a lot scientists don't know about sharks.

Scientists want to find out more about how sharks behave. Then they might find the answers to why sharks attack and what can be done to stop attacks.

They know some sharks live a long time, maybe as long as humans do, but they are not sure exactly how long sharks can live.

Scientists have made tests with sharks. They know that sharks can tell the difference between certain shapes and sizes, for example. They want to know what else sharks are able to do, and what kinds of things sharks can learn.

Scientists want to find out more about certain strange deepwater sharks that have never been seen alive, like the white goblin shark, which has a long snout shaped like a spear and vicious-looking teeth. Dead goblin sharks have been found occasionally in fishermen's nets.

Another strange shark is the frill shark, with a body shaped like an eel and frills on its throat. Very little is known about it. Scientists who have examined its teeth say that it might be able to eat slippery prey, like squid.

Scientists also want to know why most deep-sea sharks go no deeper than 6,000 feet. Their deep-sea relatives, the *chimeras,* live at 12,000 feet. Why not sharks?

How long do sharks live? Why do sharks attack? When do sharks mate? Do sharks feel pain? Do they get sick? And there are many more unanswered questions left about new species of sharks. Perhaps one day, you will work on finding the answers.

For Jim and Odile Scheiner, superb underwater photographers who study sharks the world over.

The author acknowledges with thanks the invaluable assistance given by Dr. Eugenie Clark, senior research scientist and professor emerita, University of Maryland.

No part of this publication may be reproduced in whole or in part, or stored in a retrieval system, or transmitted in any form or by any means, electronic, mechanical, photocopying, recording, or otherwise, without written permission of the publisher. For information regarding permission, write to Scholastic Inc., 555 Broadway, New York, NY 10012.

ISBN 0-590-41360-0

This is a newly illustrated and revised edition of the book *Sharks*, first published in 1976.

Book design by Laurie Williams

12 11 10 9 8 7 6 5 4 3 2 1   01   5 6 7 8 9/9 0/0

Printed in the U.S.A.   0 8